MW00709630

FLIGHT

MILITARY AIRCRAFT

June Loves

This edition first published in 2002 in the United States of America by Chelsea House Publishers, a subsidiary of Haights Cross Communications

Chelsea House Publishers
1974 Sproul Road, Suite 400
Broomall, PA 19008-0914

The Chelsea House world wide web address is www.chelseahouse.com

Library of Congress Cataloging-in-Publication Data Applied for.
ISBN 0-7910-6559-6

First published in 2000 by
Macmillan Education Australia Pty Ltd
627 Chapel Street, South Yarra, Australia, 3141

Text copyright © June Loves 2000

Edited by Lara Whitehead
Text design by if Design
Cover design by if Design
Page layout by if Design/Raul Diche
Illustrations by Lorenzo Lucia
Printed in Hong Kong

Acknowledgements
The author and the publisher are grateful to the following for permission to reproduce copyright material:

Cover: F-18 Fighter (center), courtesy of Australian Picture Library/George Hall.

Photographs courtesy of: Australian Picture Library/George Hall, pp. 22–3; Australian Picture Library/David McClenagahan, pp. 14–5; Australian Picture Library/UPPA, pp. 3 (bottom), 18–9, 20, 21, 23 (right), 24–5; Australian Picture Library/Vandystadt, p. 25 (top); Australian War Memorial, pp. 4 (bottom), 6–7, 8, 9, 10 (bottom), 16, 17, 18 (left), 28; Coo-ee Historical Picture Library, pp. 2 (right), 4–5, 10–1, 11 (bottom right), 12, 13, 15 (top); Defense Force Public Affairs Organization Queensland/Mal Lancaster, p. 26; The Photo Library/NASA/Science Photo Library, p. 27.

While every care has been taken to trace and acknowledge copyright the publishers tender their apologies for any accidental infringement where copyright has proved untraceable.

Contents

World War I airships

ALTHOUGH AIRCRAFT TODAY are largely used for peaceful travel, **aeronautical** wartime inventions played a major role in the rapid development of aircraft. Many different airships, airplanes, helicopters and even hot-air balloons were used as military aircraft.

During World War I (1914–18), aircraft were used for **reconnaissance**, to defend air space and to attack ground targets. They were also used for support services such as transporting troops, equipment and other supplies.

World War I started in 1914. Great Britain, France, Russia, Italy and the United States were known as the Allies. Germany, Austria-Hungary, Turkey and Bulgaria, who opposed the Allies, were known as the Central Powers.

At the beginning of the war, airplanes were flimsy machines made of wood and cotton material. Neither side had aircraft that were suited to wartime flying.

Today military aircraft are often used as 'peace keepers' in United Nations operations.

AIRSHIPS

Airships developed from the technology of hot-air balloons. Unlike balloons, however, they are propelled by an engine and steered with a rudder.

At the beginning of World War I, airships were useful because they could travel long distances and stay in the air for 24 hours or longer. No airplane at that time could do this. Airships were used by both sides for observation and reconnaissance duty.

Zeppelin attacks

In 1915, German-made Zeppelin airships played an important part in air combat. Giant, silent Zeppelin airships were used by the Central Powers to attack London and other parts of Britain by dropping bombs. Defending fighters soon learned to use explosive bullets that set fire to the gas-filled balloons. As this defense became more and more successful, airplanes began to take over the roles of airships.

Reconnaissance airships

Airships were used for supply duties and to observe the enemy. The crew and passengers in the airships wore parachutes so that if the airship was damaged in an attack, they could jump out of the gondola and float to safety.

This 1919 British airship was a two seater fighter and carried bomb dropping equipment.

 Flying Fact

Airships were among the first aircraft carriers. In 1925, the US Navy used airships to carry biplanes suspended under the gondolas.

World War I airplanes

RECONNAISSANCE AIRPLANES

Early in World War I, armies on both sides realized how useful airplanes could be for reconnaissance duty. Airplanes could be used to spot enemy movements and accurately direct **artillery** to targets on the ground.

Most reconnaissance aircraft had two seats, one for the pilot and one for the observer. At the beginning of the war, few pilots were armed with more than a service revolver or rifle. It was not long before the observers were given a machine gun. At first, machine guns were mounted in front of the pilot so that they could be aimed easily.

 Flying Fact

Searchlights were used to locate enemy aircraft in the dark skies as part of anti-aircraft defenses in World War I.

THE FIRST BOMBERS

The early bombers were simple two-seater planes loaded with bombs. The first bombs were small enough to be thrown out of the cockpit by the pilot or the observer. **Vanes** kept the bomb falling straight and a fuse set off the bomb when it hit the ground.

A British Handley Page 0/400 twin engine heavy bomber in 1918.

MOUNTED MACHINE GUNS

Finding a way to attach machine guns to the early airplanes for air combat was a problem. The range of fire from the guns was restricted by the spinning propeller and other parts of the plane.

In 1915, a Dutch man named Anthony Fokker, solved this problem. He designed an Interrupter Gear Mechanism that stopped the machine gun from firing when a propeller blade passed in front of the **barrel**. The Interrupter Gear Mechanism connected the propeller and the guns using a gear arrangement so bullets passed between the propeller blades. It was not perfect—some pilots shot off their own propellers.

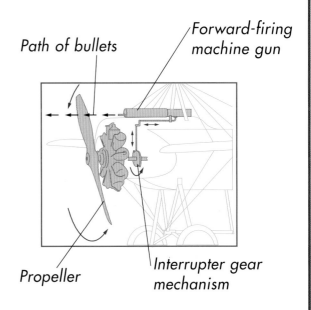

Path of bullets

Forward-firing machine gun

Propeller

Interrupter gear mechanism

BOMBER PLANES

Later in the war, larger bomber airplanes were built as the size of the bombs and their explosive power increased. Bomber airplanes such as the German twin-engine Gotha and the British Handley Page 0/400 bombers were designed to carry a heavy bomb load over a large distance.

Until 1917, the Gotha bombers flew in daylight but they were easily seen by the enemy. Successful attacks by fighters planes forced them to operate at night.

World War I fighters

SMALL, FAST FIGHTER airplanes, known as fighters, were designed and built to attack other aircraft. Fokker Dr.1 Triplanes, SE5As, Fokker E-111s and Sopwith Camels were among World War I's best fighter planes. No single type overwhelmed the others in the hundreds of **dogfights** they fought against each other.

FOKKER DR.1 TRIPLANE

The German Fokker Dr.1 Triplane was one of the best fighter planes of World War I. The triplane had a compact three-winged design that made it very easy to **maneuver** in air combat. It was the favorite aircraft of the famous fighter pilot, Baron Manfred von Richtofen, also known as the Red Baron.

SE5A

The SE5A was a British single-seat fighter of World War I. It was easier to fly than the Camel and was faster. It could fly at 193 kilometers (120 miles) per hour. It was a very stable gun platform and had a new, simple and reliable interrupter mechanism for its forward-firing synchronized Vickers gun. The SE5A was also armed with a Lewis gun mounted on the top wing that could fire forward or upward.

SOPWITH CAMEL

The Sopwith Camel was named after the shape of its humpback gun cover. The biplane was one of the most successful Allied fighters. It was extremely maneuverable and had a top speed of 182 kilometers (113 miles) per hour. Pilots flying Camels had more combat victories (1,294) than in any other type of airplane.

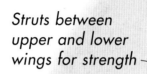

Struts between upper and lower wings for strength

Wood structure in wings

FOKKER E-111 MONOPLANE

The German Fokker E-111 wreaked havoc on Allied air forces when it introduced synchronized machine guns firing through the propeller. Some Fokkers were flown with two or three synchronized guns.

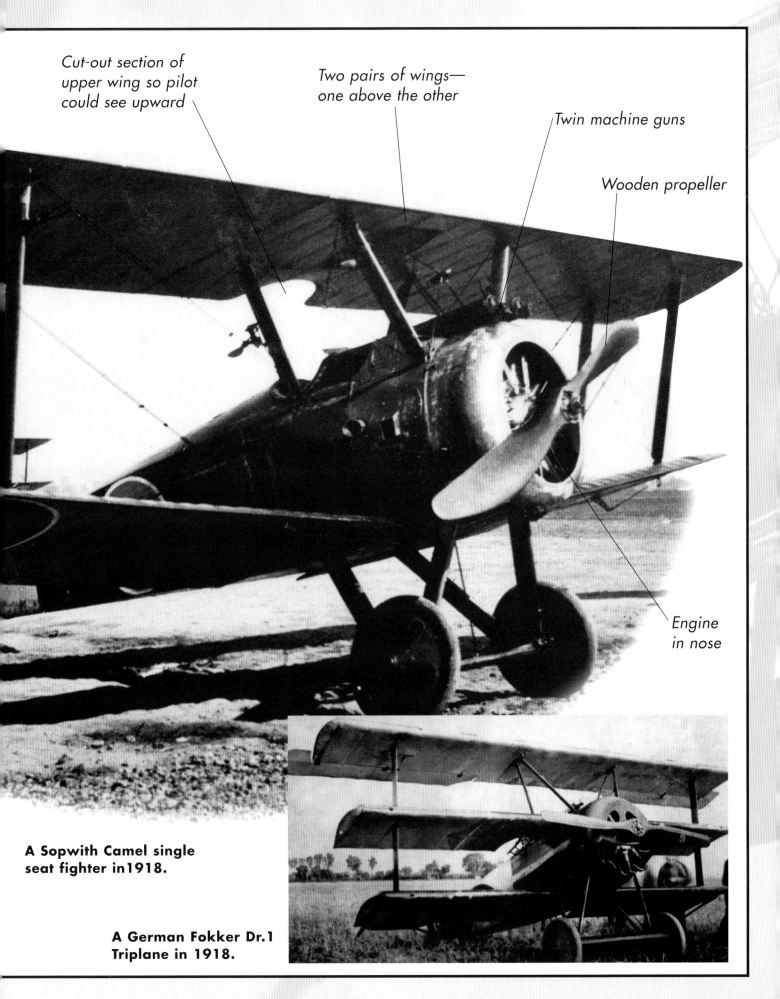

Cut-out section of
upper wing so pilot
could see upward

Two pairs of wings—
one above the other

Twin machine guns

Wooden propeller

Engine
in nose

**A Sopwith Camel single
seat fighter in 1918.**

**A German Fokker Dr.1
Triplane in 1918.**

World War I pilots

MOST YOUNG WORLD WAR I pilots received very little flight training before going into combat. However, the war turned many pilots into heroes known as 'flying aces'. The top pilots earned this title by shooting down enemy planes. The greatest air ace was the German pilot Baron Manfred von Richtofen, or the 'Red Baron'. He shot down 80 enemy planes, which was the highest tally in the war, before he died in 1918 at the age of 26.

SQUADRONS

Pilots and crew lived and fought together in teams called 'squadrons'. They often adopted a colorful symbol to distinguish their squadron from others.

FLYING GEAR

Pilots in World War I sat in open cockpits and flew in all types of weather. They sometimes flew as high as 7,000 meters (22,967 feet), where it could get very cold. In the early days of the war, the pilots wore sheepskin and leather clothing to provide warmth and protection. Goggles were essential for eye protection and boots and gloves warmed their hands and feet. Close-fitting leather helmets prevented frostbite when pilots flew at these high altitudes.

THE RED BARON

The British called Baron Manfred von Richtofen the 'Red Baron' because he painted the Albatross and the Fokker Dr.1 Triplane he flew a bright red. He also encouraged the men in his squadron to paint their machines in similar bright colors. Richtofen's 'Flying Circus' squadron was known as one of the deadliest in the sky because of its superior flying tactics and excellent planes. The Allied forces constantly worked to develop better fighters to contest them in the air.

DOGFIGHTS

Baron Manfred von Richtofen flying his Fokker Dr.1 Triplane in 1917.

During World War I, fierce air battles between two or more fighters were called dogfights. In these battles, each pilot relied on his fighting skill and plane to win. They developed **aerial maneuvers** such as loops and rolls to outperform their opponents in the air.

By 1918, most pilots flew in big formations. A single patrol could be made up of four or five squadrons. If such a patrol was attacked, huge dogfights could develop.

Flying Fact

By 1916 clothing made of waxed cotton and lined with silk and fur started to replace leather flying outfits.

A dogfight in Yres, Belgium, 1917.

Barnstorming

AIRPLANES DEVELOPED into fast, agile machines during World War I. First one side, then the other, would have temporary **supremacy** in the air as new aircraft and weapons were introduced and used in air combat. The air combat and aerial bombings of World War I changed war forever.

After World War I, Allied government forces sold their military surplus aircraft very cheaply. Pilots and airplane mechanics had to look for other kinds of work. This was the beginning of barnstorming.

Barnstorming became a popular activity as teams of veteran pilots and mechanics entertained the public as they travelled the country. They staged dogfights and took passengers up for joy rides for a small price.

Other pilots entertained the public with air shows. They showed the flying skills they had learned in the war, flying amazing aerobatics such as loop-the-loop and barrel rolls. They also performed other daring aerial stunts such as wing-walking.

BETWEEN THE WORLD WARS

In the years between the two world wars, the United States, Great Britain, France, Russia, Italy and Germany continued the development of military aircraft. When World War II was declared, government orders for military aircraft flooded into airplane manufacturers in Europe and the United States.

Famous swimmer Don Trash leaping into the water from a plane, San Diego, California, 1922.

World War II technology

IN 1939, ANOTHER world war began. World War II involved huge land, sea and air battles in many parts of the world.

Germany, Italy and Japan were known as the Axis powers. They were opposed by the Allied powers, which included Great Britain, the United States and Russia.

At the beginning of the war, many countries still had slow and lightly armed biplanes in their air forces. The pressure of gaining supremacy in the air caused new technological developments in aircraft and weapons. Airplanes became faster, weapons became more powerful, and **radar** was introduced.

By the end of the war, the first **jet** fighters were in use and devastating atomic weapons had been dropped from bomber aircraft.

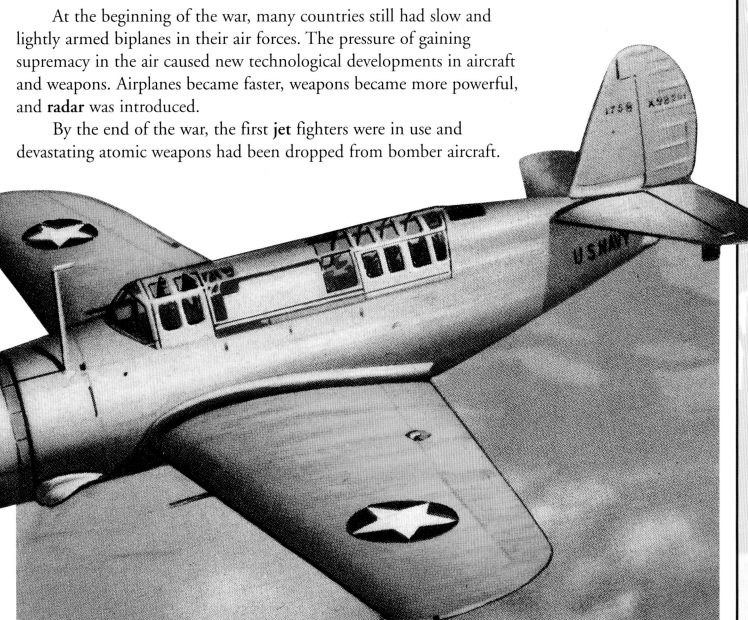

The US Curtiss dive bomber in 1945.

World War II fighters

IN SPITE OF the new, improved airplanes used in World War II, air combat was very similar to the dogfights of World War I. Whichever pilot had the faster or more agile aircraft had the advantage. Command of the air was the first step in allowing ground forces to take the territory below. Control of the air was vital for military success.

VICKERS-SUPERMARINE SPITFIRE AND HAWKER HURRICANE

Before the outbreak of World War II, new single-seater fighter airplanes such as the British Spitfire and Hurricane were developed and flew in air force squadrons. The fighters were streamlined monoplanes, armed with up to eight machine guns. The top speed of early Spitfires was about 550 kilometers (342 miles) per hour. A Hurricane's top speed was about 525 kilometers (326 miles) per hour.

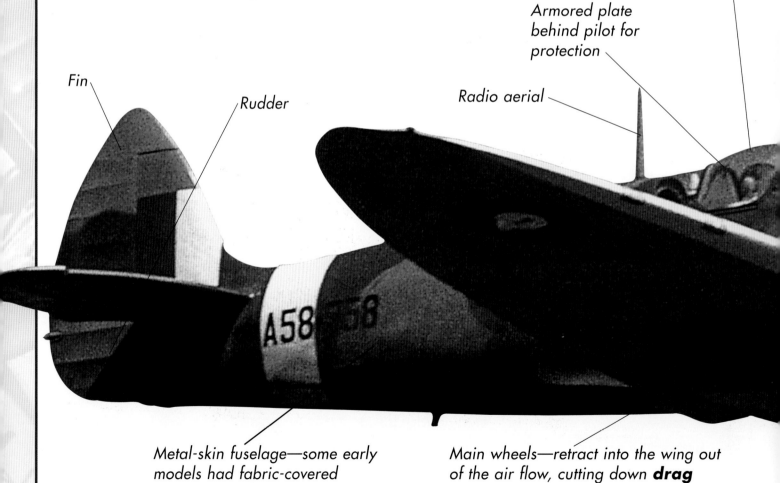

Cockpit—enclosed to shield pilot from slipstream at speed

Armored plate behind pilot for protection

Radio aerial

Fin

Rudder

Metal-skin fuselage—some early models had fabric-covered ailerons and rudders

Main wheels—retract into the wing out of the air flow, cutting down **drag** and increasing speed

GERMAN MESSERSCHMITT BF 109

The German Messerschmitt BF 109 was one of the best fighters of World War II and the most important German fighter. There were many versions but the BF 109E was most widely used in the early years of the war. It had a maximum speed of about 560 kilometers (348 miles) per hour.

A German Messerschmitt BF 109 in 1938.

Wing-mounted machine guns—early versions had eight guns, four in each wing

Powerful 12-cylinder Rolls Royce Merlin engine

Flying Fact

Streamlining cuts down drag or air resistance by helping air to flow smoothly past things.

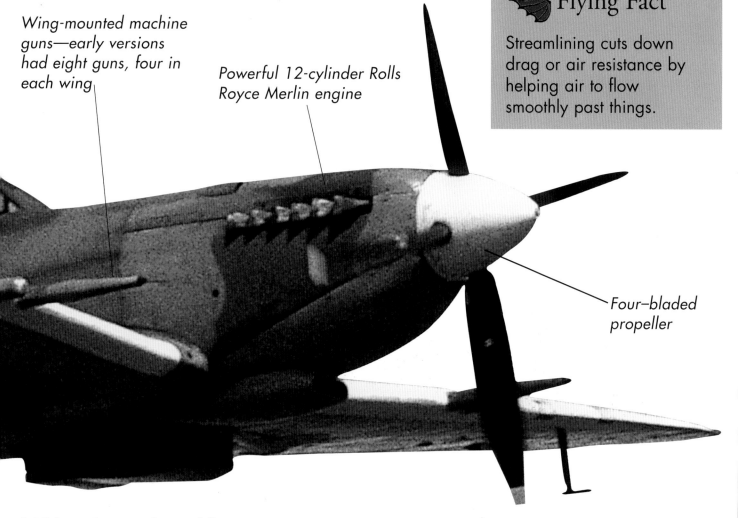

Four–bladed propeller

A Vickers-Suermarine Spitfire.

MITSUBISHI A6M ZERO

The Mitsubishi A6M Zero was designed in 1937. It was lightly built to achieve agility and was a very effective fighter aircraft in the first years of the war. Its maximum speed was about 530 kilometers (329 miles) per hour.

MACCHI C202

During World War II, Italian aircraft were not generally as advanced as machines from other countries. However, the Macchi C202 Folgore was an excellent fighter aircraft. It was fitted with a German Daimler-Benz engine and had a maximum speed of about 600 kilometers (373 miles) per hour.

P-51D MUSTANG

The P-51D Mustang one of the best fighters of World War II, provided long-range escort protection of formations of bomber aircraft.

A Mistsubishi A6M Zero.

BATTLE OF BRITAIN

The Battle of Britain was a major air battle fought in 1940. The Allies had developed new radar warning systems that enabled the Spitfires and Hurricanes to be in the air at the right time and place to engage German forces. After three months of air combat, Germany had to withdraw from 'Operation Sea Lion' and postpone plans for the invasion of Britain.

World War II bombers

BOMBERS WERE USED to strike at vital targets outside the battle zone such as military bases, weapons factories or oil refineries.

HEINKEL HE–111

The Heinkel HE-111 was a twin-engine German bomber. It had a cannon and five machine guns for defense, and had a maximum speed of 415 kilometers (258 miles) per hour.

JUNKERS JU 87

The Junkers Ju 87 (or 'Stuka') was a German dive-bomber that was very effective in the early part of the war. However, it was easily shot down by British Spitfires and Hurricanes because it provided an easy target while it was in a steady dive before releasing its bombs.

DORNIER DO–17

The Dornier Do-17 was a twin-engine German bomber. Its slim fuselage gave it the nickname the 'Flying Pencil'.

BOEING B–17

The American Boeing B-17 was called the 'Flying Fortress'. It was one of the main Allied daylight bombers. It had up to 12 machine guns and could cruise at 258 kilometers (160 miles) per hour, carrying a bomb load of over two tons. The Memphis Belle was one of the most famous B-17 bombers.

The last major attacks of World War II were bombing missions. In August 1945, atomic bombs destroyed the Japanese cities of Hiroshima and Nagasaki.

 Flying Fact

The Douglas DC-3 transport plane manufactured in the United States and Europe carried Allied troops, supplies and civilians during World War II.

A Boeing B-17.

Military helicopters

HELICOPTERS ARE **ROTARY-WINGED** aircraft that have the ability to take off and land vertically, move in any direction, and hover. Helicopters have many uses as military aircraft because of their ability to fly like this. They can be used as fighters for ground attacks, and as anti-submarine and anti-ship attack aircraft.

TROOP TRANSPORT

Helicopters are used for troop transport over land or sea. They can also move equipment, supplies and ammunition. A Chinook helicopter can hold more than 40 troops. It can also carry heavy loads of equipment slung underneath the fuselage.

A Chinook helicopter dropping supplies to troops in a remote area, Vietnam, 1970.

RECONNAISSANCE DUTY

Helicopters are often used to spot enemy movements and weapons. Some helicopters are armed with guns or rockets.

ATTACK HELICOPTERS

The modern helicopter has developed as a military fighting aircraft. It can carry rockets, missiles and cannons and is capable of seeking out and destroying enemy targets, including tanks.

The American McDonnell Douglas AH-64A Apache is a complex aircraft that was used in combat in the Gulf War in 1991.

Modern military aircraft

TODAY MANY WARS ARE fought mainly in the air. Military aircraft have many different roles in these conflicts. Fast fighter and bomber planes carry guns, missiles and bombs. Other aircraft transport troops and equipment, fly reconnaissance missions over land and sea, and refuel other aircraft in mid-air.

Modern military aircraft cost billions of dollars to design and build. They contain complex electronic systems for cockpit displays, navigation, weapons systems, surveillance and self-defense.

STRIKE AIRCRAFT

The US B-52, also called the Stratofortress, is the chief heavy bomber of the US Air Force. It is powered by eight engines and can carry conventional bombs or 20 Cruise missiles.

Strategic bombers such as the B-52 are used for striking deep into enemy territory at major targets such as military bases and nuclear missile sites. They do not have to fly over their targets but release guided missiles from a distance.

MODERN ARMAMENTS

Strike aircraft may be equipped with bombs, **air-to-surface missiles**, torpedoes or mines. Many weapons are dropped or fired and guided automatically. They can be guided by radar, laser beam or television signals. Strike aircraft may also have guns and missiles for their own protection.

MISSILES

The missiles carried by an aircraft depend on its role. Different missiles are used for air defence, ground attack or for use against ships and submarines.

Anti-aircraft missiles

Anti-aircraft missiles are fired from sea and land-based launchers, as well as from other planes. An aircraft can be brought down by a hand-held weapon such as the Javelin ground-to-air missile.

Cruise missiles

Cruise missiles fly low to avoid detection by radar. They have a complex computer system to enable them to fly a long distance with great accuracy. They can carry nuclear warheads.

Soviet SA-3 anti-aircraft missiles.

A Tomahawk Cruise missile on a test flight.

Flying Fact

The Sidewinder is a heat-seeking missile that homes in on the hot exhaust of a plane's engines.

A B-52 Stratofortress.

Fighter aircraft

DUE TO RAPID technological developments, modern fighter aircraft are very different from the fighters of World War II. To make the modern fighters more maneuverable for air combat, many are unstable and would be difficult to fly without computers. Because of this, their flight-control systems are controlled by computers to give maximum performance.

F/A 18 HORNET

The multi-role F/A 18 Hornet is one of the most effective fighter aircraft in the world. It can be used for air combat, close support of ground forces or for striking enemy targets outside the battle zone. It has a 20-millimeter (0.8 inch) cannon and can carry weapons such as the Sidewinder missile for air combat, the Harpoon anti-ship missile and conventional or laser-guided bombs.

An F/A 18 Hornet.

Type: Single-seater fighter/strike aircraft

Wingspan: 12.4 meters (40.7 feet)

Maximum speed: **Mach** 1.75

Type:	Two-seater, variable sweep fighter/attack aircraft
Wingspan:	13.9 meters (45.6 feet) 8.6 meters (28.2 feet)(swept back)
Maximum:	speed: Mach 2.2

PANAVIA TORNADO

The Panavia Tornado is a very successful, **supersonic** two-seater fighter. By fitting it with different equipment packs, it can be used for air defense, ground attack, reconnaissance or electronic warfare missions.

The Panavia Tornado is a **swing-wing** jet fighter. Fully extended, the Tornado's swing-wings allow it to take off in a distance of less than one kilometer (0.6 mile) when fully loaded. Sweeping the wings back lets the aircraft make low-level flights at supersonic speeds.

Pods containing electronics to confuse enemy missiles

Panavia Tornado.

Sidewinder short-range missiles (next to fuel tank)

Cigar-shaped tanks carry extra fuel

BRITISH AEROSPACE HARRIER

The British Aerospace Harrier, nicknamed the jump-jet, is the most versatile military fighter. It is a **subsonic** VSTOL aircraft that is designed for a vertical take-off or a very short runway. VSTOL stands for Vertical or Short Take-Off and Landing. It is a unique fighter aircraft because it can fly up or down, sideways and backwards, and even hover like a helicopter.

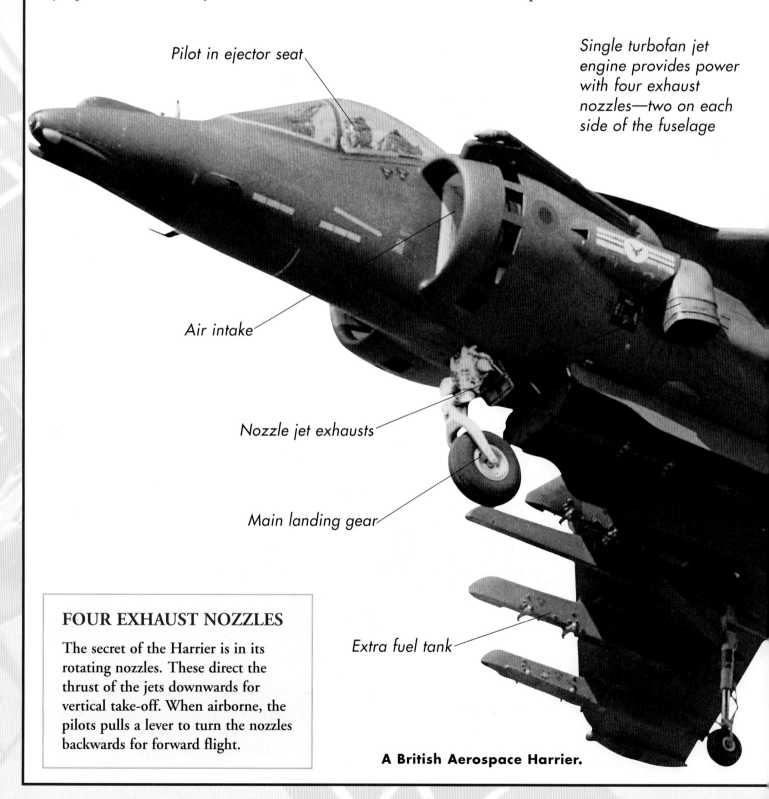

Pilot in ejector seat

Single turbofan jet engine provides power with four exhaust nozzles—two on each side of the fuselage

Air intake

Nozzle jet exhausts

Main landing gear

Extra fuel tank

FOUR EXHAUST NOZZLES

The secret of the Harrier is in its rotating nozzles. These direct the thrust of the jets downwards for vertical take-off. When airborne, the pilots pulls a lever to turn the nozzles backwards for forward flight.

A British Aerospace Harrier.

FIGHTER PILOTS

Fighter pilots are often regarded as the best in the air force and their training is long and expensive. In some air forces, fighter pilots train on a turboprop airplane to learn the basic art of flying. Then they graduate to a high-speed jet trainer, and finally convert to an actual fighter before they join a fighter squadron.

Tinted sun visor, also for high-speed ejection protection

Lightweight protective helmet with built-in radio earphones

*Outer G-suit over flying suit inflates around the waist and legs to prevent the pilot from losing consciousness during high **G-turns***

Face mask for breathing oxygen is also fitted with a radio microphone

Oxygen/radio hose

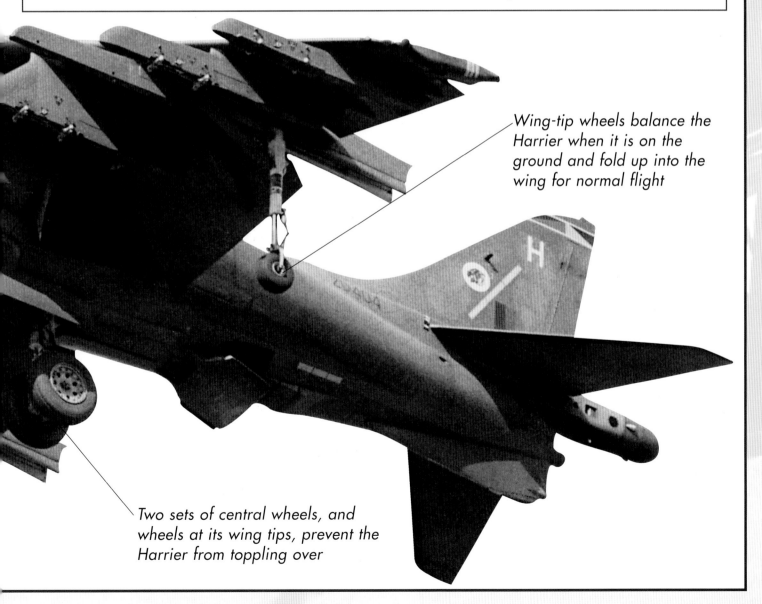

Wing-tip wheels balance the Harrier when it is on the ground and fold up into the wing for normal flight

Two sets of central wheels, and wheels at its wing tips, prevent the Harrier from toppling over

FLYING FIGHTER AIRCRAFT

Modern technology has been used to simplify the displays in the cockpit, leaving the pilot more time to look out, fly the plane and concentrate on the mission.

Large windows allow pilots to see as much as possible while they are flying.

Head-up display

A head-up display projects flight information onto a screen in front of the pilot. The information can tell the pilot the speed, direction and height of the airplane, the time to the first target, the direction of the next target, and so on. A helmet-mounted display shows the same information in front of the pilot's eyes. The pilot can look at the display or, by slightly refocusing, look through it to the outside of the cockpit.

Fingertip control

The fighter pilot usually flies with one hand on the control stick and the other on the throttle, which controls the engine's speed. In modern cockpits, there is a new system called 'Hands on Throttle and Stick' or HOTAS. Many of the controls needed for combat are grouped onto these two devices.

FIGHTER PILOT MISSIONS

Fighter pilots may fly several different types of missions such as reconnaissance, air combat, ground attack, or bomber escorts.

Reconnaissance missions

Reconnaissance missions are flown for many reasons: to gather detailed information about the position of enemy air forces, to detail movement of enemy forces, to monitor the enemy's electronic transmissions, or to assess the damage caused by attacks on enemy forces.

Reconnaissance aircraft can carry cameras, infra-red detection devices and electronic surveillance equipment. They may fly high and fast to avoid enemy **retaliation**, or low and fast to avoid radar detection. They observe the enemy movements on land, sea and in the air.

Air combat

In air combat, a fighter pilot usually tries to destroy enemy airplanes with missiles, keeping as far away from the target as possible. However, close-in dogfighting may occur between fast and maneuverable fighters. Planes climb, dive and turn, each pilot trying to hit the enemy and to protect their comrades at the same time. The result of any dogfight depends on the quality of the airplanes, their weapons and the skill of the pilots.

The Blackbird SR.71A is a high-flying reconnaissance airplane. It has powerful radar to detect in-coming enemy aircraft or missiles. It can fly at a height of 24,000 meters (78,744 feet) at three times the speed of sound.

Emergency equipment

PARACHUTES

Parachutes are designed to provide a slow descent for people or objects. The air pushing up into a parachute canopy causes drag, and slows the fall of people or objects enough to give them a safe landing.

Parachutes have many uses, from making emergency escapes from damaged aircraft, to dropping soldiers and military vehicles into enemy territory, to dropping food and medical supplies into places where there are no roads or airfields.

US Army paratroopers landing in Dutch New Guinea, 1944.

World War I parachutes

Few pilots had parachutes in World War I, even though the combat pilots may have only had a few hours of flying experience. Military commanders thought that providing parachutes would discourage bravery in the pilots.

World War II parachutes

During World War II, Allied pilots and their crews were issued with parachutes. Fighters only flew up to 700 kilometers (435 miles) per hour, and in an emergency the pilot and crew could simply jump out and open their parachutes. Pilots who parachuted into enemy territory tried to escape to friendly countries to avoid being captured and held as prisoners of war.

EJECTOR SEATS

Modern jet fighters fly so fast and things can go wrong so rapidly that it is impossible for their crews to climb out of the cockpit into the air flow. To overcome this problem, most military jet aircraft have ejector seats to fire the crew to safety.

The ejection seat is a normal seat in the airplane. However, when the pilot pulls the 'eject' handle, the seat will throw them clear of the aircraft.

HOW PARACHUTES WORK

As the parachute falls the upward force of air resistance increases and causes drag, which allows the parachute to descend slowly.

How the ejector seat works

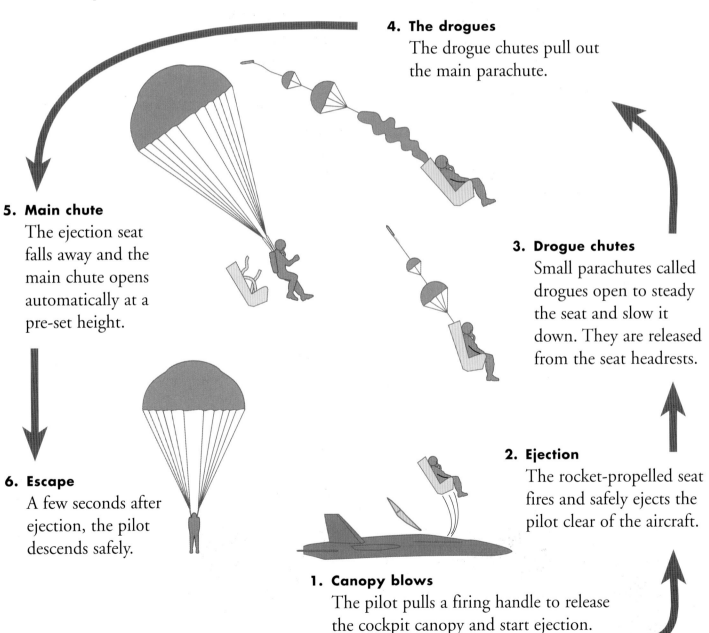

4. The drogues
The drogue chutes pull out the main parachute.

5. Main chute
The ejection seat falls away and the main chute opens automatically at a pre-set height.

3. Drogue chutes
Small parachutes called drogues open to steady the seat and slow it down. They are released from the seat headrests.

6. Escape
A few seconds after ejection, the pilot descends safely.

2. Ejection
The rocket-propelled seat fires and safely ejects the pilot clear of the aircraft.

1. Canopy blows
The pilot pulls a firing handle to release the cockpit canopy and start ejection. The canopy is blown clear of the aircraft.

Flight timeline

1783 In France the brothers Joseph and Etienne Montgolfier launch the first successful hot-air balloon.

1852 The first steam-powered airship is flown by the French engineer Henri Giffard.

1890s The German engineer Otto Lilenthal builds and flies monoplane and biplane gliders.

1903 The Wright brothers make the first powered-aircraft flight at Kitty Hawk, the United States.

1909 French pilot Louis Bleriot makes the first successful airplane flight across the English Channel.

1910 The first commercial air service is established by Count Ferdinand von Zeppelin of Germany, using airships.

1914 World War I begins. Aircraft are used on both sides.

1919 Two British pilots, John Alcock and Arthur Whitten Brown, make the first non-stop flight across the Atlantic.

1927 The US pilot Charles Lindberg flies his Spirit of St. Louis solo across the Atlantic from New York to Paris.

1930 Frank Whittle of Great Britain takes out a patent for a jet engine.

1939 The first jet aircraft, the German He178, makes its first flight.

World War II begins. Aircraft are used on both sides.

American engineer Igor Sikorsky designs the first modern helicopter.

1947 Charles 'Chuck' Yeager breaks the sound barrier in the American Bell X-1 rocket plane, the first supersonic aircraft.

1952 The world's first jet airliner, the DeHavilland Comet, enters regular passenger service in the UK.

1970 The Boeing 747 jumbo jet enters service.

1975 The supersonic Concorde, the world's fastest airliner, goes into transatlantic service.

1984 The X-29, the experimental plane, flies for the first time.

1986 Dick Rutan and Jeana Yeager make the first unrefuelled round-the-world flight in the Rutan Voyager.

1989 The B-2 Stealth bomber is test flown.

1999 Bernard Piccard and Brian Jones, a Swiss doctor and a British pilot, fly around the world in a hot-air balloon.

2000 and beyond New supersonic space planes may be flying around the world carrying passengers and cargo in record-breaking times. Airships may provide regular passenger and cargo services. The International Space Station (ISS) will be fully functional by 2004. Astronauts and scientists will commute between Earth and the ISS to live and work in space. People may be flying between Earth and outer space as they live and work in bases on the moon and other planets.

Glossary

aerial maneuver   special flying trick, such as loop-the-loop

aeronautical   having to do with flying

air-to-surface missile   a missile that is fired from an aircraft and designed to hit a target on the ground

artillery   large guns used by an army

barrel   the metal tube of a gun

dogfight   close combat between two or more fighters planes

drag   air resistance that slows an object down

G-turns   the apparent increase in weight experienced during turns

jet   a type of engine that provides thrust by a powerful exhaust. This can be a turbojet or a turbofan, which has a large front fan that also gives thrust

Mach   a measure of the speed of airplanes in relation to the speed of sound. Mach 1 is the speed of sound. Mach 2 is twice the speed of sound

maneuver   the ability to move easily

radar   a method, using special radio waves, for detecting objects such as aircraft or for locating an aircraft's own position

reconnaissance   observing the enemies' forces or territory

retaliation   to attack someone in return for their attack on you

rotary-winged   an aircraft with wings that turn in a circle, such as a helicopter

subsonic   travelling less than the speed of sound. At sea level the speed of sound is 1,225 kilometers (761.2 miles) per hour but this decreases as the plane climbs higher and the air gets thinner

supersonic   travelling faster than speed of sound

supremacy   the state of being the best at something

swing-wings   wings that can be moved backwards and forwards in flight. The different positions give the aircraft the best possible wing shapes at various speeds

vane   the blades of a propeller

Index